Good Character Press, Inc.
proudly presents

GETTING YOUR PARENTS OFF YOUR BACK…
and on your side

by

Dr. Mike Thomson

Other works by Michael M. Thomson Ph.D.

- *Dr. Mike's "Who Owns The Problem"* (poster) It's a colorful and convenient reminder of Dr. Mike's most important message.

- *Strategies for Saving Your Sanity in Parenthood* (book on cassette) ISBN: 1-883980-03-8. (book on CD) 1-883980-04-6. This is the audio edition of the book, read by Dr. Mike.

- *Strategies for Saving Your Sanity in Parenthood: Typical Problems - Practical Applications* (cassette) ISBN: 1-883980-05-4. (CD) ISBN: 1-883980-06-2. This is not a recorded version of the book. In this upbeat audio, Dr. Mike walks you through solving typical problems using his trademarked strategies.

- *Strategies for Saving Your Sanity in The Classroom* (book) ISBN: 1-883980-07-0. If you ever felt you had to teach with one hand tied behind your back, this is the book for you. It's full of common sense, hands-on strategies every teacher will love.

- *Strategies for Saving Your Sanity in The Classroom* (book on cassette) ISBN: 1-883980-08-9. (book on CD) ISBN: 1-883980-09-7. This is the audio version of the book, read by Dr. Mike.

- *Strategies for Saving Your Sanity in The Classroom: Typical Problems - Practical Applications* (cassette) ISBN: 1-883980-10-0. (CD) ISBN: 1-883980-11-9. This is not a taped version of the book. Dr. Mike, in his entertaining style, walks you through the solution to the toughest problems in education and shows you how to really save your sanity.

- *Strategies for Saving Your Sanity in Coaching* (book) ISBN: 1883980-12-7. If you are a coach at any level, this is the book for you. Full of common sense, hands-on strategies every coach will love. (Scheduled release – Fall 2003)

- *Strategies for Saving Your Sanity in Coaching: Typical Problems - Practical Applications* (cassette) ISBN: 1-883980-15-1. (CD) ISBN: 883980-16-X. Playing a sport is one thing. Coaching is altogether different. Dr. Mike shows you the blueprint for creating team success both on and off the field.

CALL 1-800-290-2482
for ordering information

Fasten Your Seatbelts...You Are Now Entering The World Of

GETTING YOUR PARENTS OFF YOUR BACK...

and on your side

With Dr. Mike

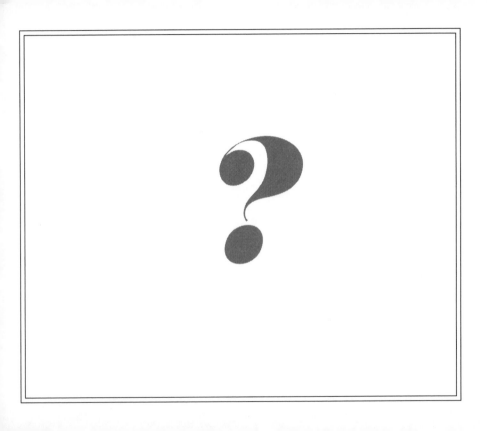

Answer these questions first:

"Are you interested in getting your parents and other adults off your back?"

"Would you like to have more power, control and choices in your life?"

"Would you like to stay up later, stay out later, have more money in your pockets and do more of what you want?"

"Would you like to be able to make more of your own decisions?"

"Would you like to have your parents trust you more?"

"Are you willing to learn some new skills to help you obtain all of the above?"

IF YOU ANSWERED "YES" TO ANY OR ALL OF THESE QUESTIONS THEN READ THIS BOOK UNTIL THE PAGES CURL UP.....................

YOU ARE REALLY RAISING YOUR PARENTS

Let's face it, parents can be a real problem. On the other hand, so can kids. Parents want kids to change. Kids want parents to change. Therein lies the problem and also the solution. Although you may not be able to change your parents, you will learn in this book that you can influence the way they treat you.

What you are holding is not just another one of those "dumb quote books." This book is a tool. A tool that will open up many different areas of your life. A tool that will stimulate your thinking about your parents, your teachers, your coaches, other adults, your friends and most of all your own life.

There are lots of books and strategies on the market for parents to change their kids but very few for kids to learn how to cope with and influence their parents. It's daring for a young person to take the initiative for a change, but you are taking that initiative by reading this book. In order to create some change at home, you, too, will have to do some of the thinking, evaluating, understanding and changing. After all, the most effective way to influence others is by changing your own behavior first.

Even though you may feel like your parents came from a different planet some days, your parents have already gone through the age you're at now, they know at least something about it. You, on the other hand, have never been an adult. In knowing this, it is critical for you to step back and understand their thoughts about what is or is not going on in your life. What you will teach your parents over the years you are around them is incredible. You'll teach them everything from love, joy, sadness, sorrow, pain, anger, patience as well as listening to name just a few.

As you are getting older you are hopefully finding out that you are actually becoming the teacher and your parents are playing the role of the students. It's now time for you to teach them what you have learned in your life up to this point. Take charge of your life just as the teacher takes charge of the classroom by showing your parents that you are becoming more responsible with each passing day. Understand, though, that a good teacher does not "control" the student but influences them with suggestions and "allows" the information to sink in. Get ready to become the "Teacher of The Year" in your home.

I have gathered within the following pages a boatload of thought tingling, humorous, and most of all practical suggestions that young people have told me they liked over the years in response to my workshops, lectures, radio talk shows and television appearances to well over 1 million people. Each section begins with my favorite anonymous sayings I've come across over the years that just get you thinking followed by suggestions that I know will help you out. Some of the suggestions you will read will give you a "kick"in the seat of the pants to get ideas into action. Some suggestions will "whack" you on the side of the head to get you out of some negative thought patterns and allow you to step back, rethink and look at what you're doing in a whole new way. Most suggestions you read will trigger an immediate response. You might look at some suggestions and think "this one doesn't have anything to do with me," or "that's stupid. I'll never think, say or do that." Don't be tempted to go on to the next suggestion. Don't do it. Force yourself to think about each one. What would be the results if you did think, say or did do what is being suggested in this book?

Now, let's get real! Will using these suggestions mean you're family life will become like the Brady Bunch? Unfortunately, no. These suggestions are not a cure-all. Stuff definitely does happen. Some moments will still be the pits. The good news, however, is that using these suggestions can dramatically change these "moments" and your outlook on life for the better. The key many say is to read and re-read this book until these suggestions become natural choices in your life. Like I said in the beginning, read this book until the pages curl right up!

Make a plan to share at least one suggestion with your parents, friends and others you come in contact with on a regular basis. This keeps you on track with a new way to think about yourself, your parents, other people and life in general. There is also no better way to learn new information than by teaching it to someone else. This brings me to another point. Some of you may be using this book within a study group. Discussing each suggestion with others and answering the questions associated with each suggestion will take you one step beyond those who read this book by themselves. However you read this book, enjoy the process steps of learning new information in your quest to get your parents (and other adults for that matter) off your back and on your side.

Everybody I've met over the years has told me that they want to be "successful" at getting their parents and other adults off their back as well as successful in life. I've always told people in my talks around the world that "It's not by chance God gave me two ears and one mouth." I've used these ears to specifically listen to what thousands of successful young people have been telling me. As a result, this book now becomes the mouthpiece for what I have learned in all of my travels. You'll discover that the key to being successful is not just "talking the talk" but in "walking the walk." As one young adult told me in one of the thousand of letters I have received over the years, "fake it till you make it if you have to!" Practicing new ideas and suggestions over and over is how successful people get where they are today. Actions do speak louder than words.

Finally, it is important for you to understand that we as parents can't possibly control all the situations you will come up against in life, but we can arm you in advance with some of the greatest gifts in life in order to avoid the pot holes of life. Since knowledge is one of the greatest gifts one can receive, read on and remind yourself how simple life can really be.

I look forward to personally meeting you someday on your journey through life.

— *Dr. Mike*

You will find the chart on the next page very useful in your journey into adulthood. It will serve as the backdrop for the information you are about to jump into. I believe that you will find yourself referring back to this chart in your self-discovery and discussions with others regarding any of the suggestions made in this book. Go ahead, try it out. Think of any problem you might be having and work your way through the questions. Try out problems like being grounded, getting a detention, getting a poor grade, getting a speeding ticket, being in a bad mood and so forth. Using these suggested questions in your life will keep you focused in the right direction. Using these questions with others will influence them to also rethink about the problem at hand. I think you will find that these six questions along with the suggestions in this book will become invaluable.

Insert The Problem Here.

Who owns the *PROBLEM?*

Who owns the *RESPONSIBILITY?*

Who made the *DECISIONS?*

Who has the *POWER?*

Who has the *CONTROL?*

Who makes the *CHOICES?*

ATTITUDE
IS
EVERYTHING

The difference between winners and losers
The winner is always part of the answer;
The loser is always part of the problem;
The winner always has a plan;
The loser always has an excuse;
The winner says, "let me do it for you;"
The loser says, "that's not my job;"
The winner sees an answer for every problem;
The loser sees more problems with every problem;
The winner sees a green near every sand trap;
The loser sees two or three sand traps near every green;
The winner says "It may be difficult, but it is possible;"
The loser says, "It may be possible, but it is too difficult;"
CHOOSE TO BE A WINNER!

— Anonymous

–1–

YOUR ATTITUDE IS THE MOST POWERFUL TOOL YOU HAVE. It will ultimately make you a success or a failure. Positive attitudes are only developed within people who practice thinking, acting and talking positive on a regular basis. Life can make you bitter or make you better...It's your choice!

"In what ways will you begin thinking positive?" "What choices can you begin making today that will demonstrate this to others?" "What are three statements that you can choose to make to others that will demonstrate that you are really serious about being a positive person?"

-2-

Don't get all twisted out of shape over something you have no control over. You can't afford to live in the land of "What if" or "Ya but." Let it go. **CHOOSE TO STEP BACK AND RETHINK, NOT REACT**. Your thinking makes the difference between a lifetime of blaming, misery and unhappiness and one of joy, happiness and acceptance. Marinating in misery is a choice you make for yourself. Ask yourself this question "How will marinating in misery help me solve the problems in my life right now?" Your thinking has the power to create and the power to destroy. *You choose.*

"What prices does a person pay when choosing blaming, misery and unhappiness?" "Why would a person make these choices?"

-3-

WHEN CHOOSING A NEGATIVE ATTITUDE, expect others around you to do less for you, not more. **YOUR ATTITUDE IS IN YOUR CONTROL**. Take a moment to ask yourself "Is my choice attitude bringing people closer to me or pushing them away from me?" "How long am I willing to keep this negative attitude?" "How is my choice to keep a negative attitude helping me to get what I want in life?"

"In what ways does a negative attitude direct the choices you make in life?" "In what ways does a negative attitude direct how you choose to feel at any given moment?"

-4-

Hopes, dreams and fantasies are the thoughts that come before getting what you want in life. If you want to make a change in your life, understand that change begins first with a change in your thinking. Ask yourself these constant and never ending questions **"AM I WILLING TO CHANGE MY ATTITUDE IN ORDER TO GET WHAT I WANT?" "AM I WILLING TO CHANGE MY ACTIONS IN ORDER TO GET WHAT I WANT?"** It's not just enough to think your way through life. You've got to get your rear in gear and make the right choices to make hopes, dreams and fantasies come true.

"What are your dreams?" "In what way is a person's attitude related to their dream coming true?"

-5-

L et your parents and other adults know that either **"REACTING TO" OR "STEPPING BACK AND RE-THINKING" A SITUATION IN LIFE IS A CHOICE YOU HAVE CONTROL OVER.** A sure sign of growing up is knowing that it is not the "situations" in life that create your responses. Maturity is knowing that it is your ability to step back and rethink the situations you are experiencing which will affect the choices you are then in control of making. Demonstrating this to adults around you will pay off. Go ahead and try it...

"What is one situation that happened recently where you 'reacted' to it?" "In what ways could you choose to step back and rethink the same situation?"

-6-

"**YOU CAN'T CLIMB UPHILL BY THINKING DOWNHILL THOUGHTS**" is a great quote. Get rid of the "Give-up-attitude" and develop the "Can do attitude." Ask yourself the questions: "What is really silly, ridiculous or downright goofy about the negative thoughts I've had?"..."What have these negative thoughts cost me?"..."What will keeping these negative thoughts in my life cost me?"

"How will asking yourself these questions help you out in life?" "What prices does one pay for "giving up?"

-7-

Developing a "Can't-stand-it-itus" attitude is a way to keep you stuck with a problem. Whenever you say that you "can't stand it," you are in fact really standing it. What you really need is a whack on the side of the head to kick start your thinking and get that brain of yours working. Instead of choosing to stay stuck, develop an **"I HAVE CONTROL OVER ME"** AND AN **"I HAVE CONTROL OVER CHANGING MYSELF" ATTITUDE.**

"What will you tell yourself next time when the 'can't-stand-it-itus' phrases come up?" "In what ways can you help others around you when they choose to use this give-up phrase?"

-8-

Don't get caught up in the attitude that if you do something to "Please" your parents that they "Owe" you something in return. **DOING SOMETHING TO GET SOMETHING WAS YOUR CHOICE.** You set yourself up for frustration if your outcomes are dependent on others responding in certain ways. It's a better choice to rethink that your choices "may influence" your parents and others in ways you desire.

"What are some choices that can influence your parents in a positive way?" "What are some choices that can influence your parents in a negative way?" "What choices have you made that have set you up for being frustrated with other humanoids?"

-9-

Whenever I ask young people if they want to be successful in life, everyone gives a resounding "Yes!" I never hear "No, I want to be a loser!" **YOU DON'T JUST HAPPEN TO STUMBLE UPON SUCCESS**. You visualize it. You see it in your "minds eye" everyday. You believe it. You want it. You plan it. You work at it. You never give up. You deserve it. You know that there are no shortcuts to success.

"What are your visions for success in life?" "In what ways is your vision for success broken down into simple steps to be taken?" "Who do you know that has what you want right now?" "What's keeping you from making some of the same choices for yourself?"

-10-

If you ever develop the negative attitude of **"I CAN DO WHATEVER I WANT TO AND WHENEVER I WANT TO,"** remember that other people always have "their own choices" in responding to you. When your choices made at the time interfere with others living their lives the way they would like to, prepare to be confronted by them. You may not like what you get in response.

"What are the consequences with hanging on to such an attitude as this?" "In what ways might parents or others react to you with an attitude such as this?"

-11-

I f you choose to have an on-going negative attitude around your parents, that's your choice. You choose the length as well as the intensity level of your attitude. Let your parents know that you really do understand why they would not give rides, money, special privileges and so on to someone who chooses such an attitude. Don't forget to mention to them that, **"ATTITUDE IS EVERY-THING."** (You'll probably have to dial 911 after they hear this from you!)

"How important is having a good attitude in life?" "In what ways does choosing to have a negative attitude affect other areas of your life?"

-12-

EVENTS DO NOT FRUSTRATE YOU, it's how you choose to think about those events. An event is not an on-going practice. It is something that happens to you and then it is over. If there is something you've said or done that was really goofy at the time, learn from it and move on. Don't repeat the goofy choice. Teach and model this to everyone you come in contact with.

"In what ways have you allowed events to really bug you?" "How can focusing on 'those events' keep you thinking, acting and feeling negative in your day to day life?"

-13-

All things in life are not what you see,
Understanding your thinking is one possible key,
To avoid extended frustration, anger and pain,
THINK POSITIVELY about things and watch
how they change.

"Besides just thinking positively, what choices does a person need to make to overcome frustration, anger and pain?" "In what ways can frustration, anger and pain be a positive experience for you?"

-14-

PEOPLE'S INTERPRETATIONS OF EVENTS ARE LIKE FINGERPRINTS–THERE ARE PLENTY OF THEM. Your parents and other adults may think about an event or something that happened in a certain way. If that is not the way you would interpret it, your job is to calmly explain your side to them in order to help them think about it differently. The key is to provide them your side of the story and your information in a calm manner. It's the best you can do to present your view.

"In what ways have you 'lost it' when trying to explain your side of a story to your parents and other adults?"
"What prices did you pay for choosing to 'lose it' with them?" *"What is a better choice to use next time?"*

-15-

Understand and accept that your parents do in fact have influence over you the majority of time while you're living at home. Your attitude as well as your actions will influence your parents in either a positive or negative way. Face the fact that your parents may not change their mind about some things in life that you might think differently about. Accept what you cannot change about your parents and change what you can in yourself. It is truly **YOUR CHOICES THAT DETERMINE YOUR PARENT'S' THOUGHTS ABOUT YOU AS WELL AS INFLUENCE THEM IN EITHER A POSITIVE OR NEGATIVE WAY.**

"What are some issues between you and your parents that you cannot change?" "What could you choose to do that will positively influence them?" "What could you choose to do that will negatively influence them?"

-16-

Communication begins with self-talk. What you say to yourself inside your head influences much of what you eventually say and do on the outside. If you ever get into negative self-talk, remind yourself that **YOUR THOUGHTS CAN BE EITHER YOUR BEST FRIEND OR YOUR WORST ENEMY.** You can choose either positive or negative self-talk.

"What are some of your negative self-talk statements you make to yourself?" "In what ways do these negative self-talk statements mess up your life?"

-17-

Don't just sit around and share your feelings over and over with another person about something frustrating in your life. What you will find out quickly is that the problem will still be there. When you are all done just sharing your feelings, you'll probably just feel pooped. **IN ORDER TO FEEL BETTER**, you must first begin to evaluate your own choices you are making at the time. Identify your choice actions you've been making as well as how you have been choosing to think. It is your thinking that jump starts the actions and in turn creates the feelings. Shakespeare stated it correctly when he said, *"There exists nothing good or bad, but thinking makes it so."*

"How has your feeling bad in life been related to the choices you have made?" "What alternative choices could you make to turn these feelings around?"

-18-

WE ARE NOT BORN WITH PREJUDICES...WE DEVELOP THEM. We are not born thinking negatively about other people or the world around us; we develop that from our experiences. If we can step back, evaluate our own present day values and question why we think, act or feel the way we do, it will make life that much less frustrating. It might also be of benefit to figure out where our thoughts, actions and feelings might have come from. It will take time and contemplation on our part, but the time will be well spent in the long run.

"What are some of your prejudices?" "In what ways does being prejudiced hold a person back in life?" "How can you turn any issue of prejudism you hear about in today's world into a learning opportunity for yourself?"

-19-

PEOPLE ARE VERY SIMILAR. Although differences are seen in skin color, hair, body shape, dress style, language, values and so forth, everyone has their own unique set of experiences, hopes and thoughts. This is what makes each person so unique. Make it a point to learn from every experience and person you encounter in life.

"Who have you met in your life that you've learned something from?" "How could meeting someone with a different ethnic background, race, language, value base and so forth affect your attitude toward life?"

-20-

S UCCESSFUL PEOPLE ARE POSITIVE PEOPLE. The attitudes and choices made by positive people are very contagious. The atmosphere that positive people create can be invigorating. These people choose to view life with a different set of eyes and ears. They love life and all of it's mysteries and opportunities. Start surrounding yourself with positive and successful people effective today.

"How are the people you hang around with influencing your thoughts and actions?" "In what ways are the people you choose to hang around with people with a positive vision in life?"

RESPONSIBILITY IS REALLY "RESPONSE-ABLE"

"A Difference"

As the old man walked the beach at dawn, he noticed a young man ahead of him picking up starfish and throwing them back into the ocean.

Finally catching up with the young man he asked him why he was doing this.

The youth responded by saying that "the stranded starfish would die if left until the morning sun."

"But the beach goes on for miles and there are thousands of starfish, how can your effort make any difference?"

The young man looked at the starfish in his hand and threw it back to the safety of the water.

"It makes a difference to this one," he said.

— *Anonymous*

-21-

We're not in Kansas anymore Dorothy! When you were younger, many adults took on your problems, responsibilities, decisions, power, control and choices. As we travel towards adulthood, life becomes a smorgasbord of choices and the menu items are the variety of choices one has in front of them each and everyday. On our trip into adulthood we need to be prepared to stand in line and make our own choices without influence from our friends, parents or others. In doing so, we then are responsible for the "choices made at the time." When you have made a poor choice, **ADMIT THAT YOU ARE RESPONSIBLE FOR MAKING THAT POOR CHOICE**. Choose to not blame your own choices made at the time on other people or events in your life. Accept the earned hassles as a result and make a decision to move on and turn this event into a learning opportunity.

"How have you blamed your own choices made on other people?" "What does a person lose when they blame their own choices on other people?"

-22-

Here's one that will really drop your parents to the floor! Tell your parents that **YOU DO NOT WANT THEM TO YELL UP THE STAIRS FOR YOU IN THE MORNING TO GET UP.** Inform them that you will demonstrate to them that you are becoming more responsible by setting your own alarm clock and getting up and getting ready by yourself. Tell them that getting up and ready for school is your responsibility in life. It will blow them away!

"How does relying on your parents to wake you up in the morning keep you from responsibility and maturity in life?"
"What other areas could you take over from your parents for something you should be doing yourself?"

-23-

Demonstrate for your parents that if you obtain the privilege to drive their car or any other car that **YOU WILL MAKE THE RIGHT CHOICE TO NOT DRINK AND DRIVE** or allow others to enter the car with alcohol or other drugs. You not only are to be in control of the car as the driver, but also what goes on inside that car. In fact, go one step further and let them know that if you choose to drink or use other drugs that you do not want them to allow you to use the car until you can prove to them that you are drug free. Think about it...when is the last time someone told you the reason everything is so great in their life is because they use alcohol and other drugs?

"What will be your plan of action if someone gets into your car who has been drinking or using other drugs?"
"What will be your plan of action if the driver of the car you planned to go home in has been drinking or using other drugs?"

-24-

Managing your own money is a part of life. Make a plan to take this part of life over as soon as possible. Demonstrate to your parents that **YOU CAN MANAGE YOUR OWN MONEY** by separating your money into three areas:

1) SMALL EXPENSES (junk food, games, movies, gas, etc.)
2) LARGE EXPENSES (school related trips, mini-vacations, special articles of clothing, other special items, further education, etc.)
3) CONTRIBUTIONS (a percentage to the church, the homeless shelter, special charities, etc.)

"What do you do to earn the money you spend?" "How would taking control of earning your own money influence your parents?" "In what ways can money management be a skill for life?"

-25-

Parents need to receive information from you on how you're doing in school. The older you get, unfortunately, the less information they receive regarding your choices at school. Grade reports come out every few months. That's a long time for parents to wait for information on how you are doing in school. **SHARE WITH YOUR PARENTS WHAT YOU ARE LEARNING IN SCHOOL** and how you are doing. It will ease their curiosity.

"What do you do to update your parents on what and how you are doing in school?" "How would choosing to share this with your parents influence them in a positive way?"

-26-

RESPECT OTHER PEOPLE'S PROPERTY. If you damage it, break it or lose it, find a way to repair it or replace it. Taking on responsibility for your own actions will demonstrate maturity and responsibility to others around you.

"Have you ever damaged or lost something that wasn't yours?" "How did you take care of your responsibility to replace it or repair it?" "If parents choose to pay for something or replace something that 'you broke', what is wrong with this choice on their part?"

-27-

Avoid lies. You know they get you into further trouble. Honesty is one of the most noble things to do and usually the most painful. That's why we don't hear that word so much. **HONESTY REALLY IS THE BEST POLICY.** Telling the truth demonstrates maturity and responsibility. Be honest with your parents and others and most of all, yourself.

"How does choosing to be honest demonstrate to others that you're becoming responsible?" "In what ways does being dishonest create more problems in your life?"

-28-

L et your parents know that you understand that **SCHOOL IS ONE OF YOUR RESPONSIBILITIES** during the day just like work might be their responsibility during the day. This include the activities of getting up on time, getting ready by yourself, paying attention in school, behaving yourself in school, doing your homework and so forth. Oh yes, responsibility in these areas means that no complaining, pouting, whining or excuses will be accepted for not following through on any of these. Productivity and success in both work and school are based on the good choices made by the person.

"How can getting up by yourself demonstrate responsibility?" "What other choices can you make regarding school that will demonstrate your responsibility and maturity?"

-29-

When your parents are not at home and the phone call is for them, **WRITE DOWN THE PERSON'S NAME AND NUMBER FOR THEM AND LEAVE IT WHERE THEY WILL SEE IT**. This not only freaks them out, it influences them in a positive way. It is these "little good deeds" in life that will pay off in so many ways in life at home as well as life away from home.

"How would doing this influence your parents?" "If you choose not to do this, how might it influence them?"

-30-

Help your parents to see the adult inside.

Help them to see where power, control, choices, decisions and responsibility reside.
Let those qualities shine and wear them with pride.
You'll be amazed at how this gets them off your back...and on your side.

"What choices have you learned that get your parents on your back?" "What choices have you learned that get your parents on your side?"

-31-

Freak your parents out by letting them know that **IF YOU CHOOSE TO OVERSLEEP FOR SCHOOL THAT THEY HAVE YOUR PERMISSION TO INFORM THE SCHOOL OF YOUR POOR CHOICE**. Sucking it up and accepting the school's consequences for your poor choice made at the time without complaining is the next step in accepting responsibility for this poor choice made at the time. Making a commitment to yourself that you will get your lazy rear in gear and out of bed on-time the next day is in your control.

" What would be most people's reaction if they overslept from school?" "In what ways have you ever been upset with your parents about a school-related responsibility that was actually yours to begin with?"

-32-

If kids speak in the woods and the parents don't hear them, are the kids still wrong? You might believe all parents don't believe kids and are just nosy. Guess what? It's true. It's part of our training as parents. Instead of brushing parents off, lying to them, keeping secrets or sneaking around to avoid getting caught at something you know down deep is wrong, which actually makes them more suspicious and nosy, do the opposite. Freak them out! MAKE IT A HABIT TO TALK WITH YOUR PARENTS AND DEMONSTRATE THE POSITIVE CHOICES that you are doing, experiencing and looking forward to in your life. **YOUR BEHAVIOR NEVER LIES!**

"How often do you just sit around and talk with your parents?" "How can choosing to do this help?" "How can brushing them off create problems in your relationship with your parents?"

-33-

"Everybody else get's to stay up and out later, It's not fair!" You may think that your present curfew stinks! Well...It's decision time for you. Fight against the present curfew and see where it gets you. If you make a poor choice to show up late for a stated curfew, it might be a good idea to **LET YOUR PARENTS KNOW THAT BECAUSE OF YOUR POOR CHOICE "YOU ARE CHOOSING" TO LOWER YOUR CURFEW UNTIL YOU CAN PROVE TO THEM THAT YOU CAN INDEED COME IN ON TIME.** Make sure that you tell them that you are not like some others kids who blame their lateness on someone or something other than themselves. With this in mind tell them you are choosing not to fall into victimhood or blamehood because of what Dr. Mike is teaching you. Get ready to perform CPR on them when they collapse to the ground. They won't know what hit them!

"Do you talk with your parents regarding what you feel is a reasonable curfew?" "In what ways are a person's choices related to the raising or lowering of a curfew?"

-34-

YOUR PERSONAL CHOICES AT HOME MAY INDICATE TO YOUR PARENTS YOUR CHOICES OUTSIDE OF THE HOME. Parents always have a fear of what you're doing away from them. Demonstrate to your parents good choices around home in order to earn your freedom away from home. Most importantly, when you do get time away from them, make the right choices. Your choices as well as your degree of freedom is in YOUR CONTROL.

"What choices do you make at home to demonstrate that you are responsible?" "What might you do to influence your parents into allowing you more freedom in your life?"

-35-

DON'T EXPECT YOUR PARENTS TO HAND MONEY TO YOU LIKE AN ALL-DAY MONEY MACHINE. Show them a plan for how you are going to earn the money you want in your life. When you do have money, demonstrate to them that you know the difference between spending money foolishly and spending it wisely. There is nothing worse than wanting something and reaching in your pocket and pulling out lint! When you're out of money, take on the responsibility for finding ways to earn it back.

"Do you complain about not having enough money?"
"How does complaining about a lack of money keep you from solving your problem?"

-36-

A solid relationship with anyone requires time, effort, compromising and sacrifice. Make a plan to **SPEND SOME TIME WITH EACH OF YOUR PARENTS ALONE** to build a better relationship. Try things like making a meal together, going shopping, grabbing an ice cream cone, playing cards or a board game, going to breakfast, lunch or dinner, taking a walk, taking a drive and so on. The better your relationship is, the more trust you'll be gaining, the more freedom you'll be allowed.

"What is your relationship right now with your parents?" "What choices can you make today to build a better relationship with your parents?"

-37-

Remember that the true definition of **RESPONSIBILITY IS MAKING CHOICES IN YOUR OWN LIFE THAT DO NOT INTERFERE WITH OTHER PEOPLE LIVING THEIR OWN LIVES.** Be conscious of others around you when making the choices you do.

"What are some poor choices you have made at the time that have been disruptive to other people?" "How are poor choices you have made been responsible for other people getting on your back?"

-38-

L et me help you understand why people blame others for their poor choices. Hold your right hand out, form it into the shape of a water pistol. Share with your parents and other adults that blamers hate to do this. They hate to admit they have only one finger pointing out and three fingers pointing back at themselves. **THE THREE FINGERS ARE POINTING BACK TO WHO REALLY OWNS THE PROBLEM, WHO REALLY HAD THE RESPONSIBILITY, WHO REALLY MADE THE DECISION, ALONG WITH WHO REALLY HAD THE POWER, CONTROL AND CHOICES AT THE TIME.** If you could read a blamer's mind at that moment, they would probably be saying "Oh Crap!"

" How does this visual aid relate to responsibility, account-ability and adulthood?" "What might a blaming person do when they learn about the three fingers pointing back to them?"

-39-

JUST LIKE A GOOD FISHERMAN, YOUR PARENTS AND OTHER ADULTS ALWAYS HAVE A HOOK IN YOU AND THEY CONTROL WHETHER THEY REEL IN THE LINE OR LET IT OUT. You on the other hand have control over your choices. Your goal should be to demonstrate to them good decision making on your part, making the right choices when it counts and demonstrating maturity and responsibility in an effort to influence them into letting the line out. As a result, your lake becomes the size of a birdbath or an ocean depending on the choices you make. Live by the motto that "You don't get the goodies unless you earn them."

"How can sharing this paragraph with your parents and other adults help?" "In what ways will sharing this paragraph with your parents also put you on notice regarding your own accountability for your own choices made?"

-40-

Let your parents and other adults know that the minute you start to blame someone or something else for why you are acting the way you are, you want them to say **"WHAT CHOICES ARE YOU RESPONSIBLE FOR IN THIS PROBLEM SITUATION?"** *or* **"HOW LONG ARE YOU GOING TO CHOOSE TO BLAME SOMEONE OR SOMETHING ELSE FOR YOUR CHOICES MADE AT THE TIME?"**

"How can using these questions help you or others out in life?" "Why would blamers hate these questions?"

-41-

Always remember that in the majority of cases **YOU HAVE TOTAL CONTROL OVER DOING OR NOT DOING WHAT OTHERS SUGGEST**. Others in the world around you just influence you with what they ask of you. Once you hear their suggestion, you own the responsibility for the results of your own choices made at that time.

"What are the prices a person pays for not even listening to another person's productive suggestions for change?"
"How does this negative attitude affect a person's thoughts, actions and feelings about life in general?"

-42-

We have all made some choices "at the time" where moments later we probably said something like "what a dumb, stupid, thing to do!" If you have lost some trust with your parents or other adults, because of one of those dumb, stupid choices, let your parents know that you understand it will take you time to get their trust back. YOU WILL **"PROVE TO THEM"** THAT YOU WILL REGAIN THEIR TRUST BY MAKING THE RIGHT CHOICES—ONE CHOICE AT A TIME, FROM THIS POINT FORWARD. Influencing others begins through demonstration of better choices on your part.

"What would your parents say if they read this?" "How can you influence your parents in allowing you to demonstrate trustworthiness through the choices you make?"

-43-

Explain to your parents and other adults that many people "Talk the talk but do not walk the walk" when it comes to saying what their going to do and actually following through with the actions necessary to accomplish their goal. MAKE SURE THAT YOUR PARENTS AND OTHER ADULTS KNOW THAT YOUR GOAL IS TO **"TALK THE TALK AND WALK THE WALK."** Saying this will really put you in control of following through and demonstrating this to them. As a result, each good choice made by you is one step closer to getting you what you want.

"When have you just talked the talk without following through?" "What prices did you pay for this choice?"

-44-

Responsible should be viewed as **RESPONSE-ABLE**. This view puts the power, control and choices where it belongs...with you! Discuss with your parents and other adults that YOU WANT THEM TO AVOID SOLVING PROBLEMS *"FOR YOU"* because it results in postponing accountability for who really owns the problem along with who really owns the solution to the problem. Plan to take on the ownership of life's daily problems. Plan to take on the personal power and the control to make the right choices for yourself.

"What problems have your parents and other adults taken on for you so far in life?" "How can this choice, on a parent's part, actually keep you from becoming more responsible?"

-45-

Unfortunately in today's world if a lot of people are doing it, people make that the new rule. **PEOPLE SOMETIMES LOWER THEIR STANDARDS SO THEY CAN NEVER SAY THEY ARE DOING A POOR JOB.** It should be the first subtle message to you that you are wimping out and giving in to the belief that you don't have the power, control and choices to make your own decisions in life. C'mon, Get A Grip and quit thinking of yourself as some helpless, powerless person here! Because people are doing it, DON'T YOU LOWER YOUR STANDARDS. Without a standard by which to measure up to, you can never under-perform. Set your standards high. View problem situations as opportunities in disguise. Evaluate your choices often. Stick to your plan to be successful in life. Never give up. **STRIVE TO BE THE BEST!**

What standards do you set for yourself at school, in sports, in co-curricular activities, in academics, for your career, in your relationships and so forth?" "In what ways can lowering your standards in these areas hurt you in your vision for success?

-46-

S ome people have appealed to the religious leaders of to-day to bend with the times with such statements as "You've got to get with the times and make changes." The religious leaders have come back with the response "We are representing the standard. We are not going to water down our teachings, our beliefs, or our doctrine so that you can feel better about sin." ABC's commentator Ted Koppel might have said it best in response to this, **"THE TEN COMMANDMENTS ARE NOT THE TEN SUGGESTIONS."** Check 'em out.

"What are your thoughts about what you have read here?"
"What role does religion play in your life?" "If people chose to live their life according to the ten commandments, what problems in today's world might not even exist?"

-47-

Ever heard the saying "A winner listens, a loser just waits until it's their turn to talk?" **If you want your parents and other adults to listen to you, ARE YOU WILLING TO LISTEN TO YOUR PARENTS AND OTHER ADULTS?** Do you give them a chance to make their point? Demonstrate to your parents and other adults you really do care by using your ears. Listening takes no special equipment or talent and can save you many tears over the years.

"In what ways have you chosen to not listen to your parents and other adults?" "What prices does one pay when they make this choice?"

-48-

When is the last time you saw a person with emphysema telling you how great tobacco has been for them? Have you ever heard a person say "The reason I'm so healthy is I smoke like a chimney?" Some proven "poor choices" can sneak right up on you and take hold of your life in a way that can be devastating for you as well as others. Demonstrate for your parents that **YOU CAN CHOOSE TO BE A NON-SMOKER**. Choose not to be a user of tobacco products and see where it gets you in life.

"What are your beliefs about the use of tobacco?" "How do these beliefs either help you or hurt you in your relationship with parents and others?"

-49-

S how me the money! Let your parents know that you do not want them to just give you money. After you wake them up from their shock from hearing this, explain to them that you prefer to **EARN YOUR ALLOWANCE OR MONEY YOU RECEIVE BASED ON WHAT YOU CHOOSE TO DO** in helping out around the house and elsewhere. Money should be earned, not given.

"What do you think your parents would say if they read this one?" "How can it become 'normal' in just expecting money to be given to you?" "What are the potential prices you can pay for keeping the belief that your parents are the First National Bank of Mom and Dad?"

-50-

Invisible is miserable. Choosing to keep your life goals to yourself allows you a chance to be invisible with others and not follow through on them. Demonstrate that you are making progress and **GOING BEYOND WHERE YOU WERE AT YESTERDAY** by informing your parents and others what positive choices you are making today to reach your goals you have set for yourself! Write down your goals and make them visible. Telling others what you are doing to get what you want makes you visible. Next time you see them, they'll probably ask you "So how is your progress coming along?"

"What goals have you made that you have not shared with others?" "How can keeping your goals a secret come around and bite you in the rear in the long run?"

-51-

A ccept the fact that some of the structure in the home, on teams, in the community, in the classroom and around the school are **UNSHAKABLE, UNBREAKABLE AND NON-NEGOTIABLE.** You may not agree with them. You might think they really stink! But once you know that they are in fact the structure for that environment, you do have the control as well as the choices. Always remember Dr. Mike's slogan "**Good Choice, Poor Choice, My Choice.**" Choose to bite the bullet and make the right choices.

"What are some rules in these areas listed that you don't like?" "Now that you know they are unshakable, unbreakable and non-negotiable, how can complaining about them direct your thoughts, actions and feelings regarding those areas listed?"

-52-

"Happiness: It's Not Your Fault!" Dr. Gary Applegate, a good friend of mine, wrote a great book *"Happiness: It's Your Choice."* You notice he believes in choices also. Unhappiness as well as happiness does not just happen to you. It is not a given. It is not automatic. Both happiness and unhappiness are earned by the choices you make either before or after an event has occurred. Let your parents know that you believe that other people and events may influence you but you have the ultimate choice to be happy or not. **YOU CREATE YOUR OWN HAPPINESS BASED ON THE CHOICES THAT YOU MAKE**.

"In what ways have you chosen to be unhappy?" "What prices do you pay for staying unhappy?"

-53-

SHARE YOUR VISIONS FOR YOUR FUTURE WITH YOUR PARENTS ON A REGULAR BASIS. Let your parents know what you want to do later on in life as well as your plan on how you're going to get there. Sit back and brainstorm what you might want to be doing, what you need to do to get what you want, and a simple plan to kick start you into gear.

"What prices do you pay for not setting in place a vision for your future?" "In what ways are the choices you make everyday critical to you in obtaining your goals?"

-54-

Demonstrate a **"GIVE TO GIVE ATTITUDE."** Give just for the sake of giving. Feel the happiness and power inside of yourself when you share with others just for the sake of sharing. Get involved with a volunteer community project, church related project or neighborhood project. Good deeds come from within and are not dependent on what "out there" does for you. Your efforts will pay off.

"In what ways are you involved in good deeds at home, school or in the community?" "How can choosing to be involved with a give-to-give attitude help you out in life?" "In what ways can choosing a give-to-get attitude set you up for big time frustration?"

-55-

REMEMBER THAT SUCCESSFUL PEOPLE MAKE THE RIGHT CHOICES, unsuccessful people make excuses. There are no dumb people, but there are dumb choices. Successful people think differently. Successful people choose to rethink instead of "react" to life's daily obstacles. Successful people view problems as opportunities for growth and learning. Successful people ask lots of questions to help them better understand problem situations. Successful people focus on "What can we learn from what has happened?"

"What are some dumb choices you have made in life?"
"How have you chosen to turn these dumb choices into learning opportunities?"

-56-

Inform your parents that friends, classmates and others around you might make **"POOR CHOICES AT THE TIME"** but that these choices do not make them "bad people." What is critical to learn from these people and their poor choices is the connection between the poor choices they made at the time and the earned consequences. Explain to your parents that you know you have the power and control to make the right choices whenever, wherever and whomever you are with. Turning these situations into opportunities to learn from for yourself is the way to go.

"What would your parents say if they read this one?" "How have you learned from other people's poor choices?"

-57-

Regardless of the various influences in life like going through a parent divorce, being adopted, living with one parent, having parents who are never there for you, having friends who make poor choices, having poor living conditions, not having enough money and so forth, people still have the power, control and choices as tough as it may seem. In the majority of cases, **PEOPLE ULTIMATELY HAVE TOTAL CONTROL OVER HOW THEY CHOOSE TO THINK, ACT AND FEEL.**

"In what ways can people use these influencing factors as excuses to not take control of their own life?" "What prices might they pay in doing so?"

-58-

As soon as you understood two times two, you couldn't believe there was a time when you didn't understand it. As soon as you understood that **MAKING THE RIGHT CHOICES BRINGS YOU POWER AND CONTROL IN YOUR LIFE**, you couldn't believe there was a time when you didn't understand it. Knowledge is Power. Power is Knowledge. Learn to Earn.

"How can knowing that you have power and control be a great thing?" "How can knowing you have power and control be a bummer to some people?"

-59-

YOU MIGHT NOT AGREE WITH THE STRUCTURE YOUR PARENTS SET WITH YOU at this point in your life. You might even think they're the goofiest people on the planet! As one young person put it, "Even when you think they're off their rocker, there's usually a reason for their madness." Cool your jets, stay calm and take a moment to step back and rethink about what their reason might be. Later in life, as you think about it, you'll most likely understand and appreciate them sticking to the structure they believed in at the time. Trust me on this one.

"What structure set by your parents do you disagree with?"
"In what ways will getting all twisted out of shape over them not changing this structure affect your day to day life?"

-60-

"I can't wait until I'm 18, then I can do whatever I want to!" Can you relate to this statement? Explain to your parents and other adults that when someone turns "18" it doesn't mean they can now magically do whatever they like. **IT JUST MEANS THEY ARE NOW AN ADULT IN THE EYE OF THE LEGAL SYSTEM.** Adult choices bring adult consequences. Bottom line, anyone can make good choices or poor choices at any age.

"In what ways can 'magical 18' thinking create problems?" "In what ways does becoming 18 bring on more responsibility, more decisions and potentially more problems for a person?"

-61-

SOME PEOPLE HAVE ALWAYS WONDERED WHY SOME FAMILIES GET ALONG SO WELL WHILE OTHERS DO NOT. Discuss and evaluate with your parents the four characteristics that make up a productive family;

1) PERMISSION TO "TALK" OPENLY WITH EACH OTHER,
2) PERMISSION TO DEMONSTRATE "TRUSTWORTHI- NESS" THROUGH BEING ALLOWED TO MAKE CHOICES,
3) PERMISSION TO "OPENLY SHARE PROBLEMS AND FEELINGS,"
4) PERMISSION TO DEMONSTRATE "LOYALTY" TO THE FAMILY EXPECTATIONS THROUGH MAKING THE RIGHT CHOICES.

"Which of the above four characteristics is your family doing well in?" "Which of the ones listed would your parents pick?"

WHO

CONTROLS

WHOM?

"God grant me the serenity to accept the things I cannot change, the courage to change the things I can, and the wisdom to know the difference."

— *Anonymous*

-62-

Where there is no choice, there is no responsibility. Where there is choice, there is responsibility. Explain to your parents and other adults that Dr. Mike believes that **PEER PRESSURE IS THE BIGGEST EXCUSE FOR NOT ACCEPTING THE RESPONSIBILITY FOR THE CHOICES YOU YOURSELF HAVE MADE.** People just offer up a smorgasbord of choices. Just like a smorgasbord, you take what you want and leave what you don't want. Everything in life is a choice.

"Who have you blamed your poor choices on in the past?"
"How would knowing that others are not in control of your choices be of value to you in life?"

-63-

Parents and other adults should not have to take on all the responsibility, make all the decisions, solve all the problems or always fix everything. You become "lazy" if they do. **THESE ARE ALL AREAS YOU SHOULD HAVE SOME INPUT AND CONTROL OVER.** The decisions you make in your own life will determine who you become as well as where you are going in life. Choose wisely.

"In what ways have you been lazy in not taking on problems that were your own?" "How do you take part in the decision making process around your home?"

-64-

How many times have you wished your parents, other people or events in your life would be different? We can't always control events or people in our lives. We can, however, control our response to them, as well as the choices we then make. **ALLOWING OTHERS TO TAKE CONTROL OF THEIR OWN LIVES AND THEIR OWN CHOICES** will amaze you at the amount of control you, yourself, will feel in your own life.

"In what ways have you been controlling with other people?" "What are the prices you pay for controlling other people?"

-65-

EVERY PERSON HAS SOMETHING TO CONTRIBUTE IN LIFE. You were born for a reason. Sit back and think about how you can contribute to life. Visualize your strengths. Use your potential to the fullest extent. What would you want people to remember you for after you leave this life?

"What are your strengths?" "What do you believe you can contribute to this world?" "If you were to die today, how would you want to be remembered?" "Are you living up to what you want said about yourself?"

-66-

"*What's wrong with this picture?*" If your relationship with another person "is your life" or "is your identity," ask yourself a very important question..."Who's really running your life?" Don't choose to think you can't live without something or someone—no matter what or who it might be. As tough as it sounds, **YOU ALWAYS HAVE THE ABILITY TO TAKE EFFECTIVE CONTROL OF YOUR OWN LIFE** regardless of circumstances.

" How does giving yourself and your identity to another person put you in a weak position?" "What prices do you pay for being over-dependent on someone else?"

-67-

I'm waiting for someone to come up to me and say that the reason they can't get ahead in life is because they are a child of a left-handed vegetarian! I mean c'mon! In looking back at your past problems, what didn't work, what went wrong, who else's fault it was, why this is happening to you, how life's unfair or why you can't get where you want to go, puts you out of focus. You can choose to stay there forever. Stop it already! Instead, get a grip and pull yourself together. Choose to change your thinking first and you'll be amazed at what happens. You only have a certain amount of energy, time, and potential to use each day. **CHOOSE TO FOCUS FORWARD**.

"In what ways have you focused on past mistakes, hardships or problems?" "What are the drawbacks in doing so?"

-68-

Parents and other adults don't have "total" control over your choices. I know you might not agree with this from time to time. But I think we can agree that **PARENTS AND OTHER ADULTS DO HAVE A CONSIDERABLE AMOUNT OF CONTROL OVER MANY OF THE THINGS YOU MAY WANT.** Make a decision as to how bad you want whatever it is you want from them. The decision here is something you have total control over. The control rests with your decisions.

"What are some of the 'things' that you want right now that you don't have?" "What choices might you make that will influence your parents in allowing you to earn what you want?"

-69-

There's a difference between being in the dog house and owning it. After making a choice, have you ever said to yourself or others "What a dumb, stupid thing to say or do?" Everybody messes up once in awhile. Explain to your parents and other adults once this happens that **YOU ARE MAKING A PLAN TO TAKE EFFECTIVE CONTROL OF YOUR LIFE** and that it will be easy for them to see it in the choices you make. **Remember, actions speak louder than words.**

"What was the last really dumb thing you said or did?"
"What did you do to make it an opportunity and move on in life and not dwell on the mistake at hand?"

-70-

Saying **"I DON'T HAVE TIME" IS REALLY AN EXCUSE.** Anything that you really want is in your control of making time to get it. If you really want it bad enough, you'll make time to get it. Focus on what you want in life versus what you don't want. Pick out what it is you want, organize the choices needed to get it and make the choices....NOW!

"What prices does one pay for using the excuse that they don't have time to do something?" "How does excuse making keep us on hold for getting what we want in life?"

-71-

Most kids hate being hassled by their parents about homework. Explain to your parents that **YOU WANT TO TAKE CONTROL OVER YOUR HOMEWORK**. Show them what you've done when they ask and demonstrate it in your grades versus them nagging at you. Think about this...Once your grades go up, the hassling stops. Who then, controls the hassling?

"What can you do to explain to your parents that you are taking control of your homework?" "What will be your plan of action if you run into problems in a certain class?"

-72-

"*Life stinks,*" "*It's not fair,*" "*I'm gonna lose my mind if things don't change,*" "*If only my parents or others would change, my life would be better.*" Many people say if it weren't for something "out there" that their life would be better. Think about it, who could disagree? Bottom line is that sometimes life does stink, can be unfair and really can be the pits! But don't ever fall victim to thinking that you have no choices after the fact. Whenever you find yourself using these phrases, keep asking yourself the question **"HOW IS THINKING LIKE THIS HELPING ME SOLVE THE PROBLEM THAT I AM EXPERIENCING?"**

"How many of the above statements have you said to yourself or others?" "What are the consequences in making these statements?"

-73-

Parents need to know how you're doing in school. **SIT DOWN WITH YOUR PARENTS AND LET THEM KNOW WHAT GRADES YOU ARE SHOOTING FOR**. Let them know your plan to obtain those grades. Break the plan into choices you'll be making on your own. Share your progress and you'll see the appreciation on your parent's face and in their attitude and treatment toward you.

"Do you know other students who are getting the grades you want in a particular class?" "Can you make a plan to watch them or ask them what choices they are making that you might not be making in your attempt to get better grades for yourself?"

-74-

Anybody who tells you that they never disagree with their parents and other adults and vice versa isn't playing with a full deck of cards. **REMEMBER THAT YOU CAN AGREE TO DISAGREE ON CERTAIN ISSUES WITH YOUR PARENTS AND OTHER ADULTS.** Instead of wasting your energy on someone or something that won't change, put your energy into changing yourself and what you have control over. Make a decision to accept the things you cannot change and move on with the things you can.

"What prices do you pay when you disagree with your parents and other adults in a negative tone or loud voice?"
"How can one present their side in a way that would be acceptable to parents or others they might disagree with?"

-75-

YOU ARE IN CONTROL OF ASKING QUESTIONS, not getting answers. You don't believe me? Ever had some-body refuse to answer your question, walk away from you when you are talking to them, roll their eyes, hang up on you or the like? Who "really" had the control? Make it your mission to really work on lowering your frustration level in relationships with other humanoids by catching yourself controlling for an-swers from others and stopping it immediately. **You will thank me for this one.**

"When was the last time you asked a question and someone did not answer you?" "How did you set yourself up for frus-tration when this occurred?" "What are the various choices a person could make when these problems occur?"

-76-

YOU ARE IN TOTAL CONTROL OVER FOLLOWING RULES OR DISOBEYING RULES. You know you don't "have to" do what others say, go to school, be tobacco, alcohol and drug free, drive the speed limit, keep your bedroom clean, have a positive attitude, be home on time, follow the athletic or co-curricular code of conduct and so forth. However, those who choose to follow rules have less people on their back. How's your life going right now?

"Who do you know that does not follow the rules?"
"What are the prices they pay with others when they choose to act this way?"

-77-

Be picky on who you look up to. **PICK ROLE MODELS THAT TEACH YOU HOW TO TAKE EFFECTIVE CONTROL OVER LIFE** by making the right choices. Look for those people who make successful choices, have a positive outlook and love life. Watch them closely. Listen to what they say and look at what they do. Make a plan to make the choices they are making that you are not presently making. Stick with it and you will be your own role model.

"Who are your role models?" "Are the role models you choose providing you with choices they make that are in line with your vision for success?"

-78-

Ever said something like "If only 'out there' would change my life would be better?" Switch your thinking from cause-effect to possible influence and you'll quit blaming not having your parents around when you wanted them, others being mean to you, not making the team and so on for your choices. Staying stuck on things that you wished "could have been" will keep you stuck in blamehood and victimhood. Rethink that NOTHING "OUT THERE" can dictate how you choose to think, act or feel. Parents, teachers, principals, coaches, employers, relatives, friends and the like may in fact influence you. However, your brain is not hooked up to theirs. **It is entirely up to you as to how you choose to think, act and feel.**

"How can a person allow a negative teacher, parent, friend, coach, employer, or others to run their life not only in a certain environment but outside that environment?" "What are the prices one would pay for doing this to themselves?"

-79-

Think about how much energy we use when we get excessively frustrated with people, events and things over which we have no control over. WHENEVER YOU WANT ANOTHER PERSON TO CHANGE remind yourself that the only person you have total control over is yourself. Accept the fact that there are some things about your parents and other adults you can't change. Sure it would be great if they changed. But if they do, that is up to them. **Get a grip and make a plan to live your own life.**

"Who do you know that spends way too much energy on changing things or people in which they have either no control over or at best just influence over?" "What are the prices you see them paying for choosing to think this way?"

-80-

You have heard that the squeaky wheel gets greased but you have also heard that the squeaky wheel gets kicked too. **GET YOUR REAR IN GEAR** and put the suggestions in this book to work in your life or be prepared!

"What prices do you pay for just reading this book and not doing anything that is suggested?" *"Pick out one suggestion that has made sense to you so far and that you are going to start using?"* *"How would making this change help you?"*

-81-

THE MORE YOU CONTROL OTHER PEOPLE, THE MORE THEY WILL RESIST AND ATTEMPT TO CONTROL YOU BACK. Being a controlling person will actually put you more out of control. Have your parents and others remind you that there are people and situations in life that you have no control over. This should help you step back and rethink versus react to those people or situations. It's O.K. to get frustrated and upset. Just don't stay there for any length of time.

"Who in your life have you been controlling for to change how they choose to think, act, or feel?" "What would be the prices you pay for making these choices?"

-82-

SCHOOL SUCCESS IS YOUR CHOICE

Which do you want an A, B or C?
All the control is yours, can you see?
To study or not, which will you take?
Your grades are earned by the choices you make!

"What choices do student's earning A's make?" "What choices do students earning D's and F's make?" "What makes the difference?"

-83-

Demonstrate to your parents and other adults that **CHOICES MADE IN THE PAST ARE IN THE PAST** and that they do not determine the choices you or anybody else will make in the future. **THE GREATEST GIFT ONE CAN ACQUIRE IS TO LEARN FROM PAST MISTAKES AND POOR CHOICES.**

"What are some past choices you have made that bug you?"
"What prices does one pay for never forgetting and never forgiving past poor choices made by others?"

-84-

Explain to your parents and other adults that **WHEN YOU USE THE WORDS "I MUST," "I HAVE TO," "I CAN'T" OR "I GIVE UP"** you want them to give you a boot in the rear and a whack on the side of the head (just kidding) to jumble your stinking thinking! Now that you've been reading this book you want them to remind you that everything you do in life is a choice on your part. You know that you not only own the choices in life but you also own the consequences that come along with those choices.

"What consequences come along with using these words listed above?" "What would happen to your thinking if you used words like 'I'm choosing to' in place of must, have to, can't and before the words give up?"

-85-

L IFE IS LIKE FLYING A PLANE. At first, you have no idea about how to do it. What you are now beginning to understand is that part of your parent's role is to take you up in the plane and give you quick lessons regarding the airplane controls. Before you kick them out of the plane, they jump with parachute in hand. You hear them repeat over and over, "It's your plane; fly it or crash it; it's your choice." You begin to realize that after your parents and other adults float down to earth in their parachutes, they now turn in their pilot wings and now become the control tower personnel that will provide you with information about your flying, but at no time will they be in that seat with you.

"What did you learn from reading this?"

-86-

THE NEXT TIME YOU HAVE A PROBLEM make three columns in your head or on paper. Title each column "control," "influence" and "no control." Ask yourself three quick questions:

1. "What do I have control over in this problem situation?"
2. "What do I have influence over in this problem situation?"
3. "What do I have no control over in this problem situation?"

"In what ways can using these three questions help you gain focus over your problems?" "How could you use these questions with others who are frustrated with a problem in their life?"

JUST

GOOD

MANNERS

Do Good Anyway

People are sometimes unreasonable, illogical, and self-centered.
Love them anyway.
If you do good, people may accuse you of selfish motives.
Do good anyway.
If you are successful, you may win false friends and true enemies.
Succeed anyway.
The good you do today may be forgotten tomorrow.
Do good anyway.
Honesty and transparency make you vulnerable.
Be honest and transparent anyway.
What you spend years building may be destroyed overnight.
Build anyway.
People who really want help may attack you if you help them.
Help them anyway.
Give the world the best you have and you may get hurt.
Give your best anyway.
The world is full of conflict.
Choose peace of mind anyway.

— *Anonymous*

-87-

L EAVE A NOTE that lets your parents know where you are and what time you will be home. While you're at it, make it a habit to leave notes like "I Love You," "Thanks For Being There For Me," and so forth. Some may call this smoozing. I just call it great manners and good choices above and beyond where most people are. After all, doing this might get them more on your side, than on your back!

"What's the advantage of doing what is being suggested here?" "What's the negative side of not doing these?"

-88-

NO BURPING, SPITTING, DISGUSTING NOISES, PICKING YOUR NOSE, DROOLING, WHINING, POUTING, COMPLAINING, KICKING, TEMPER TANTRUMMING, OR YAWNING OUT LOUD. But you already knew that. I'm just seeing if you are awake or not after reading 88 of these puppies so far.

-89-

Remember the golden rule **"Do unto others as you would like done unto yourself."** When someone you know receives special recognition, a special award or a write-up in the paper, **TAKE THE TIME TO LET THEM KNOW THAT YOU SAW IT.** A Good deed is done with nothing tangible received back other than the satisfaction inside for yourself of giving to others. How would you feel if someone did this for you?

"Is this something you do?" "In what ways is this plan of action good for you?"

-90-

When finished with a beverage with ice in it, **MAKE IT A RULE TO NOT CHEW THE ICE**. It bugs most people. If you don't believe me, ask around.

"Are you an ice cruncher?" "Who do you know that crunches ice?" "What do you think others around that person think about what they are doing?"

-91-

S wearing is really not appropriate at anytime. Swearing is usually brought on by some type of frustration a person is experiencing at the time. Believe it or not, you have control over what comes out of your mouth. Think about this, everything is legal in your mind.....it is what you say or do that gets you into trouble. **MAKE IT A HABIT TO NOT SWEAR**.

"What are the prices a person pays for swearing?" "In what ways can swearing create more problems for a person?"

-92-

When eating, remember that **IT IS JUST GOOD MANNERS TO NOT CHEW LOUD**. Food is supposed to be silent. You control the opening of your mouth as well as the smacking of your lips. Part of having good manners is being aware of others around you and what generally might be bothersome to most people.

"Do you know any lip smackers?" "What might others say about those who choose to chew loud?"

-93-

When getting out of a friend's car make it a habit to always **SAY "THANK YOU" TO THE PERSON WHO DROVE.** It's amazing what this does to influence others. If there are others in the car with you, try to be the first one that says this when getting out of the car.

"What are the payoffs in doing this?" "What is the negative side of not choosing to do this?"

-94-

When in a public place like a movie theater, restaurant, auditorium, mall and the like, be conscious of other people and their privacy. **KEEP YOUR VOICE AND YOUR BEHAVIOR AT A LEVEL THAT IS APPROPRIATE**. It's just a good habit to get yourself into at an early age. Some call it respect. Some just say it's the right thing to do.

"How could a loud voice and disruptive behaviors be bothersome to others?" "What are the potential consequences one could pay for these choices?"

-95-

If you work hard to treat others the way you wish to be treated, and are generally kind, compassionate and caring, **SOONER OR LATER YOU WILL INFLUENCE THEM.** You could always choose to go in the opposite direction and work on being "mean and nasty" to the other person. But think of the energy that this choice uses and the possible end results?

" If a person does all of the above, might another person refuse to be influenced?" "What's the benefit for you in continuing to make these choices despite how another person reacts?"

-96-

If you spill your milk, drop some food, or mess up in some way, **DON'T GET ALL BENT OUT OF SHAPE** over it, just pick it up in a calm matter of fact way. **Getting nuts over something that has already happened is really a waste of energy**. Just get it done and move on.

"What happens when a person does not pick up their messes?" "What prices can a person pay if they fall into the 'I was gonna do it, but I forgot' mode?"

-97-

G iving is no guarantee in getting anything back. **GIVE JUST FOR THE JOY OF GIVING** with no strings attached. Give a smile without getting one in return. Give a "Thank you" without getting one in return. Give a "Hi" without getting one in return. You get the picture.

"What is the problem with developing an attitude of 'giving to get' something in return?" "In what ways have you been guilty of this?"

-98-

What part of "No" don't you understand? Demonstrate to your parents that when they say "NO" to a question you ask, you really understand that "NO" IS THE FINAL WORD — don't keep asking. This may really freak them out if you have already developed a habit of always whining, complaining and not giving in when they have already answered your question.

"Are you guilty of harping on your parents after they have said 'no'?" "How would choosing to accept 'no' as the final word help you in influencing your parents in a positive way?"

-99-

MAKE A PLAN TO NOT SWEAR, SCREAM OR RAISE YOUR VOICE at your parents or other people. If you step back and rethink about it, these choices just create one more problem on top of whatever you're frustrated about. Remember, you control those lips!

"In what ways does raising your voice create one more problem whenever you are talking to someone else?"
"What prices do you pay in the short run and long run if you choose to do this?"

**SHOCKING
THE
SOCKS
OFF
YOUR
PARENTS**

I CHOOSE:

To live by choice, not by chance;
To make changes, not excuses;
To be motivated, not manipulated;
To be useful, not used;
To excel, not compete;
I choose self-esteem, not self-pity;
I choose to listen to the inner voice, not the
random opinion of others.

— *Anonymous*

-100-

S AY PLEASE AND THANK YOU on a regular basis.

"What are the positives with doing this?" "What are the consequences with not making this a habit in your life?"

-101-

When you have friends spend the day or night at your home, **CLEAN UP AFTER YOURSELVES.** Ask your friends to help.

"Would you feel comfortable asking your friends to do this?"
"Why or why not?" "How would this action on your part
influence your parents?"

-102-

PICK UP YOUR DIRTY LAUNDRY and put it where your parents want it. Better yet, ask your parents to teach you the necessary skills to doing the laundry yourself. If you end up asking them to teach you these skills, trust me, you will be going beyond where no young person has ever gone before!

"What's the advantage in doing this?" "How would doing this demonstrate personal responsibility to your parents?"

-103-

C LEAN UP THE BATHROOM after you have been in it.

"How do you feel when you are in a bathroom that's a mess?" "How would cleaning up your bathroom impress your parents?"

-104-

C LEAN UP AFTER THE FAMILY PET without being asked to.

"How does this demonstrate responsibility?" "What would your parents say if you did this?"

-105-

Here's some things you can do without your parents asking....they will love it!

CLEAN UP THE GARAGE.
CLEAN UP THE BASEMENT.
CLEAN UP THE FAMILY ROOM.
DO THE DISHES.
MOW OR CLEAN UP THE LAWN.
TAKE OUT THE TRASH.
WASH THE CAR.
SET THE TABLE.
DUST THE FURNITURE.
CLEAN THE WINDOWS.

"What are the advantages of doing any of these?"

-106-

If you choose to **PLAY MUSIC IN YOUR HOME, DO SO AT A LEVEL THAT IS BEARABLE BY YOUR PARENTS AND OTHER LIVING HUMANOIDS IN THE AREA.** We may both agree that music sounds great loud, like at the concert, but a concert setting is different than a home setting. Right?

"What would your parents say if they read this?" "What are the consequences for choosing to not do this?"

-107-

Demonstrate your independence by **MAKING YOUR OWN LUNCH** for school versus your parents making it for you.

"How does this demonstrate independence, responsibility and maturity?" "How would expecting your parents to do this keep you from moving toward adulthood?"

-108-

LET your parents know how much you care about them on a regular basis. **HUG YOUR PARENTS WITHOUT REASON**.

"How would your parents react if you were to do this?" "How would doing this influence your parents?"

-109-

MAKE YOUR BED without being asked to. Pick up your dirty laundry. Put away your clothes.

"What's your bedroom look like right now?" "How is choosing to have a clean bedroom a step toward adulthood and personal responsibility?"

-110-

Demonstrate that **THE FAMILY ROOM WAS NAMED FOR A REASON AND MAKE A PLAN TO JOIN THEM IN THERE ONCE IN AWHILE.**

"How much time do you spend talking or doing things with your parents?" "How would making a plan to spend time with them influence them in a positive way?"

-111-

SURPRISE YOUR PARENTS...set your alarm, get up on your own, get ready by yourself and make your own lunch for school.

"What would your parents reaction be to you taking on this responsibility?" "Are there any prices you pay for not doing this?"

-112-

If ever you run into your parents and other adults being on your back ask yourself the questions **"WHAT CHOICES HAVE I BEEN MAKING TO GET MY PARENTS AND OTHER ADULTS ON MY BACK?" "WHAT CHOICES AM I WILLING TO MAKE TO GET THEM OFF MY BACK ...AND ON MY SIDE?"**

"What are the advantages of answering these questions for yourself?" "What is the problem with the typical reaction of the 'it's not my fault' routine?"

-113-

Let your friends and other people around you know that your parents and other adults are not the ones that ground you, take the phone, money, stereo, car, Sega, Nintendo or favorite games away from you, give you a detention, give you a speeding ticket, put you in jail, get you booted off the team, get you fired from the job or anything else . . . **YOUR CHOICES MADE AT THE TIME WERE RESPONSIBLE FOR THE PRIVILEGES YOU HAVE LOST! YOU OWN THE CHOICES. YOU OWN THE PROBLEM.** You had the power and control to make either a good choice or a poor choice at the time but that unfortunately you made a poor choice and you are owning up to it.

"What would your parents say if you told them that because of your poor choices, you are choosing to be grounded, lose the use of the car and so forth?" "How would choosing to think this way get your parents off your back and on your side?"

**The
Only
People
Without
Problems
Are
Dead!**

Please Hear What I'm Not Saying

Please-hear what I'm not saying: Don't be fooled by the face I wear, for I wear a thousand masks. And none of them are me. Don't be fooled, for God's sake don't be fooled. I give you the impression that I'm secure, that confidence is my name and coolness is my game. And that I need no one. But don't believe me. Beneath dwells the real me in confusion, in fear, in aloneness. That's why I create a mask to hide behind, to shield me from the glance that knows, but such a glance is precisely my salvation. That is, if it's followed by acceptance, if it's followed by love. It's the only thing that can liberate me from my own self-built prison walls. I'm afraid that deep down I'm nothing, that I'm just no good. And that you will see this and reject me. And so begins the parade of masks. I idly chatter to you. I tell you everything that's really nothing and nothing of what's everything, of what's crying inside of me. Please listen carefully and try to

The Only People Without Problems Are Dead!

hear what I'm not saying. I'd really like to be genuine and spontaneous, and me. But you've got to help me. You've got to hold out your hand. Each time you're kind, and gentle, and encouraging, each time you try to understand because you really care, my hearts begins to grow wings, very feeble wings, but wings. With your sensitivity and sympathy and your power of understanding, you alone can release me from my shadow world of uncertainty, from my lonely prison. It will be easy for you. The nearer you approach me, the blinder I may strike back. But I am told that love is stronger than strong walls. And in this lies my hope, only hope. Please try to beat down these walls with firm hands. But gentle hands–for a child are very sensitive. Who am I, you may wonder? I am someone you know very well. For I am every man you meet, and I am every woman you meet, and I am you, also.

— *Anonymous*

-114-

Here's a simple fact of life – **WHAT YOU FOCUS ON IS THE DIRECTION YOU WILL GO.** Focus on your problems and they will become bigger everyday and lead you in a direction you will not be happy with. Rethinking and focusing solutions and choices that you have 100% control over will lead you into a different direction. The problems will begin to fade away.

"In what ways can you relate to what is being said here?" "In what ways do negative thoughts direct a person's life?"

-115-

Inform your parents and other adults that when you have a problem it is really an opportunity in disguise. It's an opportunity for you to first step back and look at the choices you made at the time. **IT IS ALSO AN OPPORTUNITY TO ACKNOWLEDGE AND ACCEPT THE CHOICES YOU'RE RESPONSIBLE FOR AS WELL AS THOSE THAT YOU HAVE CONTROL OVER MAKING FROM THIS POINT FORWARD.**

"How would adopting this philosophy help you in life?"
"How could choosing to not think like this affect your life?"

-116-

ARGUMENTS NEVER SOLVE ANYTHING. They just keep things at a feeling level which can really get you pooped. Both sides believe their own point of view is right. The first step in stopping an argument comes from one side taking control and choosing not to raise their voice and get into it. Sure this may require stuffing a sock in your mouth, but think of the additional problems it will save you. Talking out things without yelling and blaming is always a better option. Quit blaming the events or other people in your life for how your life has turned out. Sure "out there" may have influenced you, but it is really not the events or the people "out there," it is the "meaning" you attach to these events or people at the time.

*"Are you argumentative?" "What prices does a person pay
for being argumentative?"*

-117-

I t's been said that the man or the woman with the most toys in life always wins. Answer this question then, "When is the last time you saw a U-Haul behind the hearse?" You come in this world naked, you will go out naked. The most they will do is dress you up on the way out . . . maybe! Let your parents and other adults know that **TRUE SECURITY IN LIFE IS NOT BASED ON "HAVING THINGS" BUT IN LEARNING THE "SKILLS TO SOLVE THE DAILY PROBLEMS OF LIFE."** If you rethink of security in this way, then nobody ever can take the skills you learn in life away from you.

"How is having nice clothes, having a car, having money, having a degree, having a boyfriend or girlfriend and so forth actually become poor ways for us to put security into our lives?" "What prices do we potentially pay for relying on these choices as a pathway to meet our need for security?"

-118-

Being trusted by your parents and other adults is not really up to them. **THE TRUST THEY HAVE IN YOU IS BASED ON THE CHOICES YOU DEMONSTRATE TO THEM.** Talking the talk and not walking the walk is *your* problem. You may lie to your parents or other adults, but your behavior never lies!

"How have your choices been influenced by others?" "What is the problem with allowing others to influence your choices to the point that you make the same choices that they do?" "If others you know make poor choices at the time, can you still make the right choice?"

-119-

L ife is not a cake walk! There is no growing in life without going through some pain. Your self-esteem and sense of inner power comes from suffering through life's painful moments. **KEEP REMINDING YOURSELF THAT 98% OF LIFE'S PROBLEMS ARE GOING TO BE FRUSTRATING,** but they are not going to kill you. They are really opportunities to practice what you are learning in this book. 2% of the time you will, however, need to "react" to a situation at hand, because a person is either hurting themselves, hurting others or out of control. Many people have these figures backwards and pay significant prices for "reacting" versus "rethinking" problem situations in their life.

" What are some problem situations that you have experienced in life that you thought would be the death of you?"
"In what way did those situations turn out to be just frustrating and really not the death of you?"

-120-

DON'T JUMP TO CONCLUSIONS BEFORE YOU HAVE ALL THE INFORMATION ABOUT A PROBLEM. It's truly amazing how a set of words about what might have been said or done can be misinterpreted without checking out the story. Put your detective hat on and figure out the problem from all angles. Ask lots of questions in order to gain additional insight. You have control over asking questions to gain more information about what you have heard from others. Practice "Rethinking" versus reacting to a problem situation.

"Are you guilty of jumping to conclusions before you have all the facts?" "What are the prices for doing so?"

-121-

TAKE THE TIME TO LISTEN AND LEARN from your parents and other adults. Take a risk and share with your parents and other adults some of the hassles you've experienced or are experiencing in your life. Ask your parents and other adults for their suggestions in the solutions to some of the problems you are experiencing in life. They'll love it.

"What would your parents say if they read this one?"
"What are the advantages in sitting down with your parents and sharing with them the problems you might be having in your life?" "Could this be a way to influence them into learning the skills contained in this book?"

-122-

THE MINUTE YOU HAVE A PROBLEM ASK YOURSELF THESE 5 CRITICAL QUESTIONS:

1. What's the problem?
2. What do I want?
3. What choices have I made to solve this problem?
4. Have my choices worked enough?
5. What's my plan to solve the problem from this point forward focusing on only what I have 100% control over?

"What is the advantage in asking these questions when you experience problems in your life?" "What if a person chooses not to ask themselves these questions, what might happen?"

-123-

Remember that the key to stopping an argument with your parents or anyone else is **FINDING A COMPROMISE YOU CAN BOTH AGREE UPON**. There are four areas that you need to know that you have total control over in communicating with other humanoids that will help here: **1)** You have total control over demonstrating caring, **2)** You have total control over asking questions, **3)** You have total control over making statements and **4)** You have total control over discussing alternative choices available. The way in which you present your ideas to your parents makes all the difference in the world. Tone of voice on your part is the key to being heard. This can sometimes be the toughest part.

"What are the advantages of compromising with your parents or anyone else when you both can't reach a firm agreement?" "In what ways is your tone of voice critical to a compromise?"

-124-

Work on limiting yourself to a two minute rule on ventilating your feelings about your problems. Give yourself two minutes to "get it out," and then make a decision that your two minutes are up. **JUST TALKING ABOUT THE PROBLEM ON A FEELINGS LEVEL WILL KEEP IT A PROBLEM. Get a Grip, Get a Life, Get Going!** Moving on to listing the options to solve the problem is the next step. Putting those options into action completes the problem solving process.

"In what ways have you talked a problem to death?" "What are the prices you pay in choosing to do this?"

-125-

Discuss with your parents and other adults that when you have a problem to solve that you are taking the problem and breaking it down into:

1. **SIMPLE STEPS** that you have control over. (something easy)
2. **SPECIFIC STEPS** that you are going to take. (what, when, where, who, and how)
3. **A "DO" PLAN** as opposed to a STOP plan. (start something)
4. **IMMEDIATE STEPS** (put into place right now)
5. **INDEPENDENT** (dependent on what you do and not on what others do or don't do)
6. **WRITTEN** (visible to others about what you plan to do)

"What are the advantages for breaking down problems into these steps, putting them in black and white and then posting them where they can be seen by yourself as well as others?"

-126-

Personal responsibility as well as happiness in life is never someone else's responsibility. Choosing not to believe this promotes unhappiness in so many areas of your life. People are not making or keeping you unhappy. You do that to your-self. Focusing on **WHAT YOU HAVE TOTAL CONTROL OVER AND MAKING A PLAN TO MOVE BEYOND WHERE YOU ARE AT WITH A PROBLEM IS CRITICAL.**

"In what ways have you allowed other people to take on your responsibility for your life choices?" "Have you been guilty of staying unhappy because of what other people have said or done to you?"

-127-

Discuss with **YOUR PARENTS AND OTHER ADULTS THAT YOU ARE REALLY SERIOUS ABOUT TAKING ON AND SOLVING YOUR OWN PROBLEMS**. Inform them what you are working on in changing either the way you think or the choices you have been making. Explain to them that you're going to be demonstrating to them choices that show responsibility, maturity and a pathway to adulthood on your part.

"What would happen if you shared with your parents some of the suggestions from this book that you plan on putting into your life?" "How would doing this help you out?"

-128-

Ever said "I'm so angry I could just scream" about some thing that has happened in your life? Answer two questions, "How long has it been since that event occurred?" "How long are you going to stay angry?" Rethink with me that from now on you don't get angry . . . you choose "angering" as your best choice at the time to deal with frustration at hand. **ANGERING ABOUT A PROBLEM THAT YOU HAVE JUST KEEPS YOU AWAY FROM SOLVING THE PROBLEM.** Live by the motto that "There is only one solution to a problem and that is me. My choices will either solve the problem or keep it a problem."

"When was the last time you were 'angering' about something?" "Does choosing to stay angry about something that has already happened help you out in solving the problems at hand?"

-129-

When it comes to making any changes in life, many people have lots of excuses for not following through with their plan for change. This also includes the excuse of being lazy, or what you now know as being "lazying." You've probably heard the saying "Today is the first day of the rest of your life." With the start of each new day you have the opportunity to start with a clean slate. **RETHINK ABOUT LIFE IN THIS WAY...YOU HAVE 1440 MINUTES OF EACH DAY TO MAKE THE RIGHT CHOICES. CHOOSE WISELY.** What will you be doing in the next few minutes?

"Have you known someone who is really lazy?" "What are the prices for choosing to be lazy?"

-130-

You know that you can lose trust very quickly. You also know that IT TAKES TIME TO EARN BACK TRUST. **The reason we have another day in our life is to move on and learn from where we have been the day before.** Learn from each day and each experience and carve out a path for the next day. The path to being trusted usually begins with the new decision to make the right choices today.

" What's your plan to make and demonstrate better choices?" "What are the advantages in sharing this with your parents?"

-131-

If your privileges and freedoms it turns out that you miss, Ask yourself, "Which of my poor choices could have caused this?" SWITCH YOUR THINKING FROM **CAUSE AND EFFECT** TO **SOME PEOPLE AND SOME THINGS IN LIFE JUST INFLUENCE YOU.** This switch in thinking will keep you from a victimhood and blamehood thinking mode and move you into adulthood thinking. It will also impress your parents and others around you like you can't begin to imagine.

"What are the prices a person pays for falling into victimhood and blamehood?" "Why is it actually an easier choice to choose victimhood and blamehood as an excuse for some people?"

"CHOICES"

IS
NOT
A
DIRTY
WORD

Risk

To laugh is to risk appearing the fool.

To weep is to risk appearing sentimental.

To reach out for another is to risk involvement.

To expose feelings is to risk exposing your true self.

To play your ideas, your dreams, before the crowd is to risk their loss.

To love is to risk not being loved in return.

To live is to risk dying.

To hope is to risk despair.

To try is to risk failure.

But risk must be taken, because the greatest hazard in life is to risk nothing.

The person who risks nothing, does nothing, has nothing, and is nothing.

He may avoid suffering and sorrow, but he simply

cannot learn, feel, change, grow, or love.

Chained by his certitude's, he is a slave.

He has forfeited freedom.

Only a person who risks...is free.

— *Anonymous*

-132-

Parents and other adults really get freaked out about what goes on at some parties. Let's face it, they're probably justified. Discuss with them that **PARTIES ARE NOT THE ISSUE, THE CHOICES YOU MAKE AT THE PARTIES ARE THE ISSUE.** Demonstrate to your parents and other adults that you can make the right choices even when others don't.

"Why is peer pressure the biggest excuse we use for the choices we actually make?" "What would your parents say to this one?"

-133-

Punching, hitting, or kicking others is a way to create one more problem in life besides whatever a person is upset about. Some people say "I just couldn't help it," "I was having a bad day," or "they made me do it." These are just excuses that keep a person from focusing on the choices they are responsible for. Sure, the situation they experienced frustrated them, but it did not pick the choices to deal with the frustration. **BETWEEN THE URGE TO DO IT AND DOING IT, THERE IS CHOICE.** You choose to punch. You choose to hit. You choose to kick.

"Have you ever been guilty of punching, hitting or kicking?" "What are the possible consequences for a person making these poor choices at the time?"

-134-

Parents and other adults get concerned about the hair styles and dress styles that young people choose today. **DISCUSS AND DEMONSTRATE TO THEM THAT HAIR STYLES AND DRESS STYLES DO NOT DETERMINE THE CHOICES ONE MAKES.** A person could have the wildest clothes, the funkiest hair or look like the preppiest kid on the block. Those choices do not tell us what kinds of choices they make in the bigger picture of life. The real key is in what they "actually do" at the time and not in what they wear.

"How can hair and dress style have nothing to do with what a person is really like down deep?" "In what ways does hair and dress style affect another person's thoughts and actions towards that person, fairly or unfairly?"

-135-

S ome people "choose" to stay stuck in life. Unfortunately, some people like it when other people step in and make decisions for them and end up helping them out with "their problem." Do you know anyone like this? Think about it, all this really does is relieve that person from the responsibility of doing it for themselves. There are three choices whenever you feel stuck:

1. Stay stuck with the problem and give up.
2. Make negative choices that will create even more problems.
3. RETHINK and make positive choices that you have 100% control over and will move you forward in life.

"In what ways is choosing to stay stuck a poor choice?"
"Why do you think people would choose to stay stuck with a problem they have?"

-136-

G uilt is really a message from inside ourselves that we're off track. Guilt starts and ends with our thinking. Guilt informs us that it is time for us to evaluate our choices we have been making up to this point. There is appropriate and inappropriate guilt. Everybody has made poor choices at the time and as a result has felt guilty. The big question is "How long should you feel guilty?" HAS EXCESSIVELY FEELING GUILTY over something that has "already happened" ever lead you to a better choice? One young person told me that "Excessive guilt is a wasted emotion." What do you think?

"Why is excessive guilting a wasted choice?" "Is guilt over something that has already happened necessary?"

-137-

S ome parents and other adults get all twisted out of shape about the issue of sex and young people to-day. This area is definitely one that the consequences for those choosing it are different that those staying out past curfew. Nobody has ever had sex, become pregnant, shoplifted, drank, used other drugs, or been expelled by mistake! **DISCUSS AND DEMONSTRATE TO PARENTS AND OTHER ADULTS THAT A PERSON HAS TOTAL CONTROL OF ALL THE PARTS OF THEIR BODY THAT CAN GET THEM INTO TROUBLE.** Enough said!

" Do you know what decision you are going to make when it comes to sexual involvement?" "In what ways can the act of sex really ruin a relationship and get in the way of how much someone really cares about another person?"

-138-

WHINERS ARE WIENERS. Ask yourself "How does whining help me solve the problems I'm having?" People may start out whining, then move to pouting, then depressing and so forth as a way to deal with "their frustration" at the time. Whining, pouting and depressing are just places to hide when you don't want to take responsibility for yourself. **Get a grip, Get a life, Get going!**

"Have either you or someone you have known been guilty of whining?" "What prices does one pay for this choice?"

-139-

KEEP ASKING YOURSELF THESE QUESTIONS:

"How bad do I want what I want?"
"How bad do I want to be trusted?"
"How bad do I want extra money?"
"How bad do I want the use of the car?"
"How bad do I want a ride somewhere?"
"How bad do I want a sleepover?"
"How bad do I want to stay up later?"
"How bad do I want to stay out later?"
"How bad do I want to be involved in athletics
or co-curricular activities?"

GOOD CHOICES WILL HELP YOU GET WHAT YOU WANT!

*"Why would it be important to ask these questions of your-self?" "How would asking these questions in this way hold
you accountable for what you want?"*

-140-

Explain to your parents and other adults that **GETTING PHYSICAL WITH ANOTHER PERSON DOES NOT PROVE ANYTHING.** In fact it just brings one more problem into your life. There is always somebody out there with more physical strength than you. Where the real strength comes from takes place between your ears and knowing when to hold back any type of violence between you and another person. After all, that brain of yours is not just there to keep your ears from collapsing!

"In what ways do you agree with what is said here?" "What are some of the prices you or others have paid if they let their emotions and not their brain take over their decision at the time?"

-141-

By in large, People are not depressed, they are depressing. People are not bored, they are boring. People are not angry, they are angering. People are not miserable, they are miserabling. Demonstrate for your parents and other adults that you know that they are not your entertainment committee or cheerleading group. **YOU HAVE THE ABILITY TO CREATE YOUR OWN FUN, HAPPINESS AND ENJOYMENT IN LIFE.**

"Why is there an 'ing' after each of the choices listed above?"
"How would thinking and talking like this actually give you a whack on the side of the head the next time you are making those choices?"

-142-

Music is the heart and soul of everyone. You can choose to listen to a wide variety of options. **SHARE WITH YOUR PARENTS AND OTHER ADULTS WHY YOU LIKE THE MUSIC YOU DO.** Share with them what you learn from the lyrics you choose to listen to and how those lyrics are influencing you in making better choices in life.

"In what ways does music influence people?" "What are the positive and negative influences of music on how a person chooses to think, act and feel?"

-143-

Want to take a risk? Want to go beyond where no young person has gone before? Want to have a couple of hours away from your parents and the house all to yourself? Inform your parents that **YOU UNDERSTAND WHY YOU DO NOT DESERVE A RIDE TO SCHOOL OR ELSEWHERE WHEN YOU DON'T HAVE THE RIGHT ATTITUDE OR MAKE THE RIGHT CHOICES. (Be prepared to dial 911 when they hear this one! You will probably have the house all to yourself when the ambulance leaves...)**

"How is attitude in life worth a million dollars?" "What makes attitude toward life and others so important as it relates to actions and feelings a person chooses?"

-144-

Feelings like anger, sadness, pain, hurt and rejection have the ability to frustrate you, but **THE CHOICE TO "RE-ACT" IN A NEGATIVE WAY OR "RETHINK" IN A POSI-TIVE WAY IS YOURS TO MAKE.** Allow yourself to experience these feelings. Use the two-minute rule and talk about these feelings briefly and then take from the experience what you can to move forward in life. Going beyond two minutes just keeps you on hold as if "out there" is supposed to change. If "out there" does not change, who is left to change?

"How have you turned anyone of these choices listed above into opportunities in your life?" "How can staying stuck on each one of these choices hold you back in life?"

-145-

HOTHEADS ARE AIRHEADS. Ask yourself two questions:

1. "How does choosing angering help me solve my problems?"
2. "How long am I going to choose to yell and get upset?"

Hotheads are usually "hot" over people or events that they have either no control over or at best just influence over.

"Who do you know that is a hothead?" "What prices do they pay for this choice?"

-146-

Remember that "DOING YOUR OWN THING" WITH NO THOUGHT OR CONSIDERATION FOR OTHER PEOPLE is irresponsible choice making.

" Have you ever been guilty of doing this?" "Who do you know that chooses to act like this and what prices do they pay for doing so?"

-147-

We might think that many times in life our choices at the time really stink . . . but the bottom line is that we still have choices. Choosing to not do anything is a choice. It is easier than changing. It takes no effort. It's also just a watered down version of "I give up." Let your parents and other adults know that when you say something like "I give up" or "I don't have to" that you want them to come back with "you're right, you can give up and you don't have to do anything–those will always be your choices. Answer the question "How will choosing to do nothing help you get what you want in your life?" Remember that **"YOUR CHOICES CAN RESULT IN EITHER GOOD OR POOR OUTCOMES—IT'S YOUR CHOICE—IT'S YOUR DECISION."**

"What would your parents say if they read this one?" "How would hearing this advice from your parents or others be a real boot in the rear?"

-148-

Discuss with your parents and other adults that **POUTING, WHINING AND COMPLAINING ARE SUBTLE WAYS OF GIVING-UP** and that you want them to remind you to "cut-it-out" and make a better choice.

"What is the best way to get you off of pouting, whining and complaining?" "What suggestions for getting you off of these poor choices will you share with your parents and others?"

-149-

MATURITY AND RESPONSIBILITY ARE EARNED. They come from a person earning it based on the past choices they make. Good choices made over a period of time add up just like coins in a piggy bank.

"How many good choice coins do you have in your bank?" "Is the amount of coins in the bank related to your choices or other people's choices?" "If someone loses some coins due to poor choices made at the time, how can they begin to earn them back?"

-150-

You are not going to be anything you don't want to choose to be. It won't be your parents, coaches, teachers or friends who make you the way you are today. Face it, the choices are yours to make! Please don't forget some of the key points in this book like "Good Choice...Poor Choice...My Choice," "Three Fingers Pointing Back To Me," "Problems Are Opportunities In Disguise," "Rethinking Versus Reacting," "Focusing On What You Have 100% Control Over," "Trust Is Earned By The Choices You Make," and regardless of influences in my life "The Direction Of My Life Is Up To Me." **SHARE WITH YOUR PARENTS THE CONCEPTS AND SUGGESTIONS PROVIDED IN THIS BOOK.** See which ones they agree or disagree with. **Discussing these suggestions with parents opens up some great conversations** .

What are some of the key points that you have picked up from reading all of these suggestions?" "How can putting these suggestions into your life make you a better person?" "How can modeling these suggestions to others around us make this world a better place?

IF ALL ELSE FAILS

If all else fails you can always lay on your bed and dream about reversing roles with your parents:

➤ Remind them about what life was like for you in "the old days."

➤ Start every sentence with *"Well in my day.."*

➤ Remind them that money does not grow on trees.

➤ Remind them that if they don't finish their meal they're not having dessert.

➤ Inform them that they are not going out until their room is clean.

➤ Make sure they keep hearing *"If I've told you once, I've told you a thousand times"* over and over again.

➤ Complain about the clothes they wear and the style of their hair.

➤ Make the statement *"You're not going out of the house dressed like that"* at least once a week.

➤ Tell them *"As long as you live under my roof, you'll follow my rules."*

➤ Put them to bed early.

➤ Send them to their room and remind them to *"think about what they did wrong."*

If all else fails, take a trip with them and

➤ Put them in the back seat.

➤ Make sure you control the heat and the music.

➤ Set down the ground rules before you leave the driveway:
       1. keep hands to yourself.
       2. no faces.
       3. no sticking out tongues.
       4. no feet on the seats.
       5. no weird obnoxious noises.
       6. no talking.
       7. no kicking the seats.

➤ Tell them that above all *"We're all going to have a good time if it kills us!"*

➤ Threaten to turn the car around if they don't grow up.

YATS ESOOL!

(spell it backwards.....)

Thank You!
Dr. Mike

Dear Reader:

We would personally love to receive feedback from you as to how you have used this book either with others in a study group or how it has helped you personally rethink some areas of your life. We would also like to hear about additional good advice you have received from others along the way that you would like to give to other young people.

Please let Dr. Mike know of any errors, omissions, misspellings, additional questions, or additional words to help a suggestion read better. Dr. Mike would love to hear about a suggestion of your own that you feel needs to be in here for the next edition.

For information on additional books, audio and video tapes, a dynamic student assembly, athlete, coach, teacher or parent program in your area by Dr. Mike:

VISIT:

www.itsallaboutcharacter.com

CALL:

1-800-290-2482